DISNEY's

First Year Book

2003

FERN L. MAMBERG — *Executive Editor*
ELIZABETH A. DeBELLA — *Designer*
KATHERINE M. SIEPIETOSKI — *Production Manager*

Articles designed by Pisaza Design Studio Ltd.
Stories and crafts illustrated by Alvin S. White Studio.

ISBN: 0-7172-1106-1
ISSN: 0273-1274

Illustration Credits and Acknowledgments

6: The Granger Collection. 7: The Granger Collection. 8: © Maresa Pryor/Animals Animals;
© Matt Bradley/Bruce Coleman Inc. 9: Photo by Nick Galante/NASA; Photo Network; NASA/
AP/Wide World Photos. 10: © Ray Coleman/Photo Researchers, Inc.; © Lawrence Migdale/ Photo
Researchers, Inc.; © Tim Fitzharris/Minden Pictures; © John Shaw/Bruce Coleman Inc.
11: © Michelle D. Bridwell/PhotoEdit. 12: © Skip Moody; © Tim Fitzharris/Minden Pictures;
© Robert K. Grubbs/Photo Network. 13: © Michael Lustbader/Photo Reseachers, Inc.; © Gay
Bumgarner/Photo Network; © Valerie Giles/Photo Researchers, Inc.; © Gary Retherford/Photo
Researchers, Inc. © Kent Foster/Photo Researchers, Inc. 28: © Tim Davis/Photo Researchers, Inc.
29: Gerard Lacz/ Animals Animals. 30: © Joe McDonald/Bruce Coleman Inc. 31: © M.P. Kahl/Bruce
Coleman Inc. 32: © Stephan J. Krasemann/Photo Researchers, Inc. 33: © Farrell Grehan/Photo
Researchers, Inc. 46: © Bob Firth/ImageState. 47: © Jack Wilburn/Animals Animals; © Ken Frick/
ImageState. 48: © Mark E. Gibson/Image Finders; © Phyllis Picardi/Photo Network. 49: © Mark E.
Gibson/Image Finders. 50: © Luis Viega/Image Bank/Getty Images. 51: © Richard Nowitz.
52: © Wendell E. Wilson; © Luis Viega/Image Bank/Getty Images; © Jeff Scovil. 53: © Charles D.
Winters/Photo Researchers, Inc.; © E.R. Degginger/Animals Animals; © Michael Freeman/Corbis;
© Breck P. Kent/Animals Animals. 54: © Charles D. Winters/Photo Researchers, Inc.; © Jeff Scovil;
© E.R. Degginger/Animals Animals. 55: © Charles D. Winters/Photo Researchers, Inc.; © Jeff
Scovil; © Richard T. Nowitz/Photo Researchers, Inc. 70: © Toby Talbot/ AP/Wide World Pictures.
71: © Richard Hutchings/PhotoEdit. 73: top, all © Richard Nowitz; bottom, © Richard Wahlstrom/
Image Bank/Getty Images. 74: © A&M Shah/Animals Animals; © Patti Murray/Animals Animals;
© Norbert Rosing/NGS Image Collection. 75: © Tom & Therisa Stack/Tom Stack & Associates;
©Mike Anich/ImageState; © Frans Lanting/Minden Pictures; © Breck P. Kent/Animals Animals.
88: © Howard Miller/Photo Researchers, Inc. 89: © Nuridsany and Perennou/Photo Researchers,
Inc. 90: © Joe McDonald/Bruce Coleman Inc.; © John Shaw/ Bruce Coleman Inc. 91: © James R.
Fisher/Photo Researchers, Inc; © Norm Thomas/Photo Researchers, Inc.; © Breck P. Kent/Earth
Scenes. 92-93: © A & L Sinibaldi/Stone/Getty Images. 94: © Novastock/Photo Network; © Asahi
Shimbun, Takeo Kato/AP/Wide World Photos; © Werner Bertsch/Bruce Coleman Inc. 94-95: © Raj
Kamal/Animals Animals. 95: © Mary M. Steinbacher/PhotoEdit.

Disney's First Year Book 2003

SCHOLASTIC INC.

New York • Toronto • London • Auckland • Sydney •
Mexico City • New Delhi • Hong Kong • Buenos Aires

Contents

100 Years of Flight

Wilbur Wright watches as his brother Orville takes their plane, the *Flyer*, on its first flight in 1903.

On December 17, 1903, a small airplane took off at Kitty Hawk, North Carolina. The plane flew for just 12 seconds. But it made history. It was the first successful airplane flight!

Two brothers, Orville and Wilbur Wright, built that plane. The year 2003 marks the 100th anniversary of their feat. People everywhere are celebrating 100 years of flight.

People have always wanted to fly. Long ago, they watched birds fly and thought, "I wish I could do that!" But no one figured out how to do it before Orville and Wilbur Wright came along.

Until then, only balloons and gliders had carried people into the air. Balloons are lighter than air, so they rise. But they must go where the wind takes them. A glider is like a plane without an engine. It coasts on the air. And it goes only as far as it can coast.

The Wright brothers' plane, the *Flyer*, was different. It had an engine. The engine could keep the plane flying. And the plane could be steered. People could fly where they wanted to go, not just where the wind took them!

With Orville on board, the *Flyer* went only about 120 feet on its first flight. But the Wright brothers and others began to build planes that could fly much farther.

Wings of Wax

Long ago, people wondered if humans could fly like birds. A Greek myth tells how two people tried.

Daedalus and his son, Icarus, were locked in a tower by the king of Crete. Daedalus thought they could fly to freedom. He made two sets of wings, using feathers held together with wax. He put one set on Icarus, and he tied the other set on himself.

The wings worked! Daedalus and Icarus flew out of their prison. But then Icarus grew too bold. He ignored his father's warnings and flew higher and higher. He flew so high that the heat of the sun melted the wax in his wings! As the wax melted, the feathers fell out. And Icarus fell into the sea.

EARLY PLANE

FLYING BOAT

Before long, planes were carrying mail between cities. Then they began to carry passengers. As planes flew farther and faster, they began to cross countries and oceans. The first plane to cross the Atlantic Ocean was a flying boat—a plane that could take off and land on water. Way back then, in 1919, it took a plane more than sixteen hours to make the ocean crossing!

Today, big passenger jets cross the Atlantic Ocean in just about six hours. Air travel has made it easy for people to take trips to far-off places. People are still trying to fly higher, faster, and farther, too. New kinds of aircraft, like the space shuttle, even take people into space and back.

This odd plane looks as if it couldn't get off the ground! But it has flown higher than any other aircraft, except the rockets that go into space. The plane is called *Helios*. It has no pilot—it's a robot plane. It's really just a giant flying wing with five propellers. The propellers are powered by energy from the sun. Scientists built *Helios* to fly in the highest part of the atmosphere, where other planes can't go.

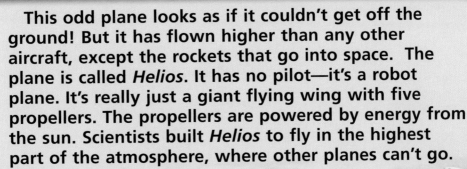

PASSENGER JET

Higher! Faster! Farther!

SPACE SHUTTLE

Life would be very different today if the Wright brothers had never built their wonderful airplane!

B Is for Butterfly

Can a flower fly? Of course not! But colorful butterflies look like flying flowers. Their wings have enough pretty colors and designs to fill a garden. That's why butterflies are among the insects that people love best. And these beautiful insects are found all over the world, except in the very coldest places.

There are about 20,000 kinds of butterflies in the world! And each kind has its own colors and patterns.

Some butterflies have bright colors and bold patterns. Their flashy wings help them find mates. It's easy for them to spot other butterflies of the same type.

Other butterflies are dull brown or gray. Their drab colors and speckles blend in with tree bark and other things in nature. That helps them hide from enemies.

Some butterflies have it both ways. Their wings are dull on one side and bright on the other. They can hide and flash their colors, too!

This is fun!

Butterfly Houses

Imagine that you are in a garden. Butterflies swirl all around you. One even lands on your shoulder!

That might happen if you visit a walk-through butterfly house. You can find these centers at zoos and some botanical gardens and museums.

A butterfly house is a big greenhouse or, sometimes, a tentlike building covered with netting. Inside are butterflies and plants from all over the world.

Butterfly or Moth?

A butterfly usually:

- Has a thin body
- Has thin antennae with rounded tips
- Flies in daylight

A moth usually:

- Has a plump body
- Has wide, feathery antennae
- Flies at night

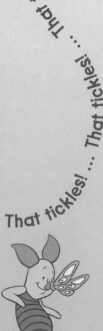

If you have ever touched a butterfly's wing, you may have seen fine dust on your finger. The dust is made up of tiny scales. Rows and rows of scales cover a butterfly's wings. The scales give the wings their colors and patterns. The scales come off very easily, and that helps the insect. If a butterfly lands in a spider's web, some of its scales may stick. But the butterfly can get away. It flies off, leaving some of its scales behind.

When you see a butterfly, flowers are usually close by. Most butterflies feed on nectar. Nectar is a sweet liquid in the center of flowers. Butterflies find their favorite flowers by sight and smell. Like other insects, a butterfly smells with its feelers, or antennae.

And a butterfly can taste with its feet! So when it lands on a flower, it quickly knows if it will find a tasty meal. If the flower seems good, the butterfly unrolls its long, coiled tongue to reach the nectar in the center. Then the insect sucks up its meal.

Most butterflies live for just a few weeks during spring and summer. During that time, these beautiful insects bring joy to all who see them.

Butterflies have lovely colors and patterns!

Scared Silly

"Hey, Sulley, you're number one!"

"Go, champ!"

"You're the best!"

The big blue monster's friends and neighbors were cheering for him. He and his best pal, Mike, were on their way to work at Monsters, Inc.

My pal is the best Scarer in all of Monstropolis, the one-eyed green monster thought proudly.

While Sulley did his warm-up scare exercises, Mike brought out a door to a child's room. Then he put a scream canister in place and waited for the light to flash. As soon as the light signaled, Sulley ran through the door into a child's room.

"Grrrr!" Sulley growled as the door was closing.

"AAAAAAAh!" Mike heard a kid scream.

"Wow, listen to that!" Mike said. Sometimes he wondered what it would be like to be a top Scarer like Sulley.

That night he told that to his girlfriend, Celia.

"Oh, Schmoopsie-poo, you're a *funny* monster," she said. "You couldn't scare a flea!"

However, Mike was determined. He'd show her. He'd show everyone that he could be scary, just like Sulley.

The next day, Mike was carrying a big bag to work.
"What's in the bag?" Sulley asked.
"I'm not telling," Mike answered.
Sulley was a little bit hurt by Mike's attitude.

Mike waited until Sulley went through a door. Then he pulled a purple fright wig and two great big shoes with claws out of the bag.

"Boo!" he shouted when Sulley dashed back through the door.

"Aaah!" Sulley yelled. Thud! He tripped over Mike's shoes. "What did you do that for?" he asked, rubbing the bump on his head.

"Did I scare you?" Mike asked.

"No, but you sure surprised me!" Sulley replied.

"Oh." Mike was disappointed, but he wasn't going to give up.

That night, Mike left work without Sulley. The big blue monster had to walk home alone. He wondered why his pal hadn't waited for him.

When Sulley got home, the apartment was dark.

"Mike, where are you?" Sulley called.

"Woooooooooo!" a strange voice wailed. Mike jumped out from behind the kitchen door. He was smeared with gooey red tomato sauce from head to toe. Slimy spaghetti trailed off his ears and dangled from his fingers.

"I'm a noodle monster!" he screeched.

Sulley started to laugh. He laughed so hard, he had to sit down.

Mike stared at his friend. "I guess that means you weren't scared," he said finally.

Sulley was gasping. "No, but you sure are funny!"

Mike stomped into his bedroom and closed the door. Sulley stood outside.

"Come on, Mike. Open up!" Sulley called, knocking on the door.

"Go away," Mike answered back.

That night, Sulley had to eat dinner and watch TV without his best friend to keep him company.

The next morning, when Sulley woke up, Mike was gone. Sulley had to walk to work by himself. He felt lonely and sad. Why was Mike acting so strangely? Was he mad about something?

Sulley went to the locker room to get ready for work. But he didn't feel much like doing his job. He was too worried about the way Mike was acting.

Just as Sulley opened his locker door, *BAM!* Mike jumped out. He was painted blue and covered with fur, just like Sulley. He was wearing stilts to make himself as tall as Sulley.

"Aw, Mike, what's wrong with you?" Sulley asked. "Why are you making fun of me? I thought you were my friend."

Sulley's feelings were really hurt. He hurried down to the Scare Floor. Mike clumped after Sulley on his stilts.

"Stop! Come back, Sulley," he yelled. "Look at me! I'm scary like you!"

All the other monsters at Monsters, Inc. stopped what they were doing and began to follow Mike and Sulley.

"What a joker!" they shouted. "Mike, you're the funniest! We're going to bust our fangs laughing!"

"I'm not funny, I'm scary!" Mike exclaimed. He took a huge breath. "Watch this!"

"RRRRrrrrrr!" Mike roared. (Some roar, huh?)

"EEEEEEEE!" Mike shrieked as his stilts flew out from under him.

"Ow-wow-wow!" Mike groaned as he hit the floor and rolled over and over.

"Ha, ha, ha!" all the monsters shouted with laughter.

Mike rolled to a stop beside Sulley's gigantic feet. He sat up with a moan and rubbed his head.

"Mike, are you all right?" Sulley asked. "What are you trying to do?"

"I wanted to see if I could scare someone," Mike explained, "but I'm no good at it." The little green monster's one eye drooped. "See! Everyone's laughing. Nobody looks scared."

Sulley helped his pal stand up. "Look, Mike, that's what everyone likes about you. You make them laugh," he said. "Besides, you sure had *me* scared!"

"Oh, sure," Mike grumbled. "How?"

"Well, it's like this, Mike," Sulley answered. "I thought you were going to quit being my best pal. And that's just about the scariest thing I could ever imagine."

Mike gently punched his pal's arm. Together they strolled down the hall. "Quit being your best pal?" Mike exclaimed. "Aw, Sulley, don't make me laugh!"

MAKING A MONSTER

Boo met lots of monster friends during her visit to Monsters, Inc. Now help her make some monster toys! (Store them in your closet to make them feel at home when you're not playing with them.)

WHAT YOU NEED

Construction Paper

Pipe Cleaners

Two Styrofoam Balls

Googly Eyes (big and small)

Colored Markers

Plastic Spoon

White Glue

Scissors

Glue

WHAT YOU DO

MIKE WAZOWSKI

* Color a Styrofoam ball with the green marker.
* Glue one big googly eye to the upper part of the ball.
* Cut out a mouth shape from construction paper. Draw teeth and a tongue on it. Glue the mouth under the eye.
* Add arms, legs, and horns by sticking pipe cleaners into the ball.

OOGLY-BOOGLY MONSTER

This monster has a few more horns—and one more eye— than Mike.

* Color a Styrofoam ball a particularly monstrous color.
* Glue two googly eyes to the front of the ball.
* Add arms, legs, and lots of horns by sticking pipe cleaners into the ball.

CELIA

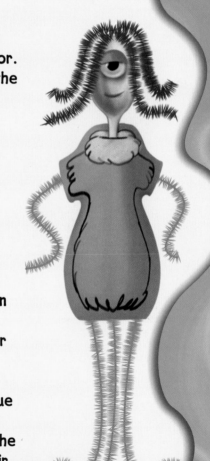

Mike's schmoopsie-poo is very particular about her hair (which is really a bunch of snakes!).

* Draw Celia's dress on a piece of construction paper. Cut it out.
* Place a spoon behind the dress, creating her head. Glue the spoon handle to the dress.
* Glue one googly eye to the spoon.
* Use pipe cleaners for arms and legs, and glue them behind the dress.
* Cut, bend, and glue more pipe cleaners to the top of the spoon to create Celia's snaky hair.

Why Animals Do What They Do!

Chimpanzees smile. Wolves howl. Rattlesnakes rattle. Elephants take mud baths. Did you ever wonder why animals do some of the funny things they do? The answers may surprise you!

Aren't you my cousin George...?

Why do chimps smile?

Look at that grin! This chimp sure looks happy. Maybe you're wondering what the joke is. But the chimp isn't laughing at all. Chimps grin like this when they are scared! The grin comes along with a loud scream. Like people, chimps show lots of different feelings in their faces. But they don't show their feelings in the same ways that people do. If this chimp were *really* happy, he would stick out his chin, show only his lower teeth, and grunt. That's how chimps laugh.

Why do wolves howl?

A wolf's howl can send shivers up your spine. The howl starts out as a low moan. It rises higher and higher. Then other wolves join in, all howling together. Are the wolves howling at the moon? Are they singing? Are they trying to scare people?

Wolves in the same pack often howl together in the evening and early morning. This "group howl" is a warning to other packs. Each pack has a territory—an area where that pack hunts. The group howl says, "We're here! This is our turf!"

A wolf howls alone when it is separated from its pack. If other pack members hear, they howl back. Howling is how wolves keep in touch with each other.

Wolves are like family to me.

First you hear a clicking sound. The clicking gets faster, until it sounds like the hiss of steam. Better pay attention! That's the sound of a rattlesnake's rattle. Many people are afraid of rattlesnakes. They think the rattle means that the snake is about to attack and bite. But the rattlesnake would rather rattle than fight!

The rattlesnake's rattle is on its tail. It shakes its rattle to warn away enemies. Rattling may save the snake from being stepped on by a horse or attacked by a dog. If it can, the snake will slither off to safety. But if it is cornered or surprised, it may bite. People are bitten when they step on snakes or try to get too close to them.

Sssssnake, rattle, 'n' roll!

Don't forget to wash behind your ears!

Why do elephants take mud baths?

Elephants love mud! In Africa, a whole group of these giant animals will sometimes join together for a mud bath. The elephants sit in the mud. They lie down and stretch out in the mud. Then they roll over on their backs. They make lots of noise as they wallow around in the goo. It's clear that the elephants are having a great time!

Elephants don't take mud baths because they like to be dirty. They do it because rolling in cool, wet mud is a great way for the animals to cool off on a hot afternoon. Taking a mud bath also soothes itching. And when the bath is over, the elephants are covered with a layer of mud. That layer protects the animals' skin from the hot sun and from biting flies and other pesky bugs. No wonder elephants love mud!

Why do raccoons wash their food?

Raccoons will eat almost anything, even garbage that people have put in trashcans. But a raccoon's favorite hunting ground is along the banks of a stream. There, the raccoon looks for snails, crayfish, and other small water animals. And it dunks and scrubs whatever it finds in the shallow water before it eats.

The raccoon seems to be washing its food. But the dunking is really just the way the animal hunts. The raccoon uses its front paws to dig in the sand on the bottom of the stream. It feels every handful of sand until it finds something to eat. Then it turns the food this way and that in its paws. Finally the raccoon pops the treat into its mouth. Yum!

Why do baby swans follow their mother?

Have you ever seen a family of swans, geese, or ducks? On land, the baby birds waddle along in a line behind their mother. In the water, they swim behind her, paddling hard to keep up. They follow their mother wherever she goes. They have been doing this ever since the day they hatched.

These baby birds are all able to run around soon after they hatch. But they don't run just anywhere. They are born with the urge to follow. Usually the mother bird is the first thing they see, so they learn to follow her. This keeps them safe and teaches them to know their own kind.

Follow me!

Briar Rose to the Rescue

Briar Rose awoke with a sleepy yawn and stretch. She looked out the window of her little room in the cottage. How delightful! It looked like spring!

After she had dressed, Briar Rose went to the kitchen to greet her three aunts—Flora, Fauna, and Merryweather.

"Good morning, dear!" called Flora.

"It's the first day of spring!" Fauna said.

"You slept late again," Merryweather grumbled, but she placed a biscuit with extra honey at Briar Rose's place at the table. Briar Rose smiled. Merryweather liked to sound grumpy, but Briar Rose knew she loved her.

"I suppose we have to do our spring cleaning today," Merryweather added.

"Yes, dear," replied Fauna. "That's what we always do on the first day of spring."

"I'm afraid we're going to need a new broom," Flora said suddenly. "This old one is quite ragged and dirty from all of our winter cleaning."

"Why don't I make a new broom?" Briar Rose offered. "I'll go out and find some straw, and a nice, straight, sturdy stick."

"Why, that's very sweet of you!" said Flora.

"Dress warmly, my dear," added Fauna. "It's still cold out, you know."

"Don't stay out long," Merryweather said. "You'll leave all the work for us!"

Briar Rose tried hard not to giggle. She knew that Merryweather wasn't worried about the work. She was worried about Briar Rose's safety.

Briar Rose wrapped her cloak around her, picked up her basket, and stepped out the door.

"Don't go trying to walk on the ice!" Merryweather shouted after her. "It can break easily, now that it's melting."

Of course, Briar Rose already knew how dangerous springtime could be in the woods. Big chunks of snow could fall from trees, and dangerously thin ice would cover the pond.

In the shed, Briar Rose gathered straw for her new broom. As she put it into her basket, two little chipmunks appeared and began to chatter at her.

"Well, come on, then," she invited. The chipmunks jumped into her basket.

Then some cheery
bluebirds chirped at her from the
rafters. "You come, too," said Briar
Rose. They were joined by other birds and animals.
Soon all the friends were parading happily through
the woods.

As they got closer to the pond, Briar Rose noticed a
flutter of activity. She stopped singing and started
worrying just a little. What could be causing such a
commotion?

The bluebirds flew on ahead to see what was going
on. Briar Rose raced after them, with Merryweather's

warning echoing in her head: *Don't go trying to walk on the ice! It can break easily, now that it's melting.*

Sure enough, Merryweather had been right. When Briar Rose approached the pond, the chipmunks started chattering. They jumped out of the basket and joined a group of animals gathered around the pond. They were looking at a deer who had fallen through the ice. The poor thing was struggling, but it couldn't get out!

Briar Rose knew this deer well. It was a doe, and she was going to give birth very soon. Briar Rose knew she had to help the doe. But how?

Thinking quickly, Briar Rose hurried over to a fallen tree nearby. She broke off a long, sturdy branch and stretched it toward the deer. The deer tried to reach the branch but was so panicked she was losing her strength. Briar Rose wondered what she could do to calm the deer.

Suddenly she had an idea. She began to sing the softest, most soothing lullaby she could think of. Soon the doe began to calm down. Then the tired creature was able to grasp the branch in her mouth. Briar Rose tugged and pulled until, at last, the doe was able to climb up onto the bank of the pond.

Briar Rose sighed with relief—until she realized how hard the deer was shaking!

"Oh, you poor thing!" cried Briar Rose. "You're half frozen!" She pulled a big handful of straw from her basket and began to rub it briskly over the deer's body. The doe's coat was beginning to dry, but she was still shivering.

"Come on, everyone!" Briar Rose said. She and the other

animals led the deer through the woods. When they reached her aunts' cottage, they burst through the front door. Briar Rose led the doe directly to the warm fireplace, leaving a trail of muddy hoofprints all over the floor.

"Oh, my!" cried Flora.

"We'll have to clean all over again," said Fauna.

"Oh, phooey!" said Merryweather. "Who cares about all that? How can we help, Briar Rose?"

"She fell through the—" Briar Rose started to say.

"Humph! I told you something like that would happen," Merryweather interrupted.

"We need to get her warm—" continued Briar Rose.

"And dry, and fed!" Once again Merryweather interrupted. "Now step to it, ladies!"

Flora, Fauna, Merryweather, and Briar Rose worked together to make the deer comfortable. A little later that spring, the doe gave birth to not one, but two beautiful fawns.

Every morning, Briar Rose would go to the shed to begin her chores. She always noticed that someone had been there before her. And that person had brought the doe and fawns a special treat. Can you guess who it was?

It was Merryweather!

Silly Scarecrows

Farmers put up scarecrows to keep birds away from their fields. But these stuffed characters are more fun than scary!

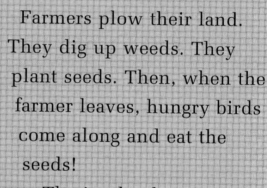

Farmers plow their land. They dig up weeds. They plant seeds. Then, when the farmer leaves, hungry birds come along and eat the seeds!

That's why, long ago, farmers began to put up scarecrows. Scarecrows are made out of old clothes, stuffed full of straw or rags. These stuffed figures are mounted on sticks and left out in farm fields.

A scarecrow is supposed to fool birds and other animals. Hungry critters are meant to think that a real person is in the field. And this is supposed to scare them away.

However, most scarecrows don't really work very well. Birds may fly away from the stuffed figure at first. But the scarecrow never moves. It always stands in the same place. Before long, the birds get used to seeing the scarecrow. They stop worrying about it. And then they go back to eating the seeds or crops that are growing in the farmer's field.

Loud noises do a better job of chasing birds away. Nowadays farmers sometimes use firecrackers or even loudspeakers to scare birds away from their fields. But people still make scarecrows, just for the fun of it!

For some people, making scarecrows is like creating a work of art. They take part in scarecrow contests that are held in towns across the United States. These contests are usually held in the fall. Prizes are handed out for the cleverest and most original designs. And some of the entries are really far out!

Most scarecrows still start with some old clothes that are stuffed with straw, leaves, or rags. The cheerful chap on the left is a good example.

But a scarecrow doesn't have to wear old clothes. Take a look at the scarecrow above. Burlap flour sacks, a garbage-can lid, old tools, and machine parts make up this funny fellow!

Just about anything can be used to make a scarecrow, it seems. The friendly farmer on the right is made mostly of cardboard tubes!

If you are in the country this fall, look for scarecrows in farm fields and vegetable gardens. Who knows what silly scarecrow characters you might see!

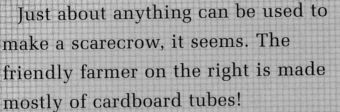

Make a Scarecrow!

To make a scarecrow, you'll need old clothes, straw or other stuffing, a bucket or a plastic pumpkin for the head, heavy string, and two sticks—one long and one short.

1. Tie the short stick to the long stick to form a cross.
2. Slip the long stick through one pant leg. Put a shirt or jacket around the "arms" of the short stick.
3. Stuff the pants and shirt.
4. Put the head on top of the long stick. Draw or paint a face. Add a hat.
5. Dig a hole and stand the scarecrow in it. Pack the dirt down around the stick.

BIRTHDAY GEMS

Do you know your birthstone? Maybe it's a glittery diamond. Maybe it's a beautiful blue sapphire. Whatever month you were born in, there's a birthstone—a special gem—for that month. And that gem could be a lucky charm for you!

Pairing special gems with months of the year is a very old idea. The gems that we use today start with deep red garnets in January. The last month, December, is paired with turquoise. The months in between are linked with jewels in every color you can think of.

Another old idea is that wearing your birthstone will bring you good fortune. And long ago, people thought that colored gems had magical powers. Even today there are lots of legends about these jewels. We know such stories aren't true—but they are fun to think about.

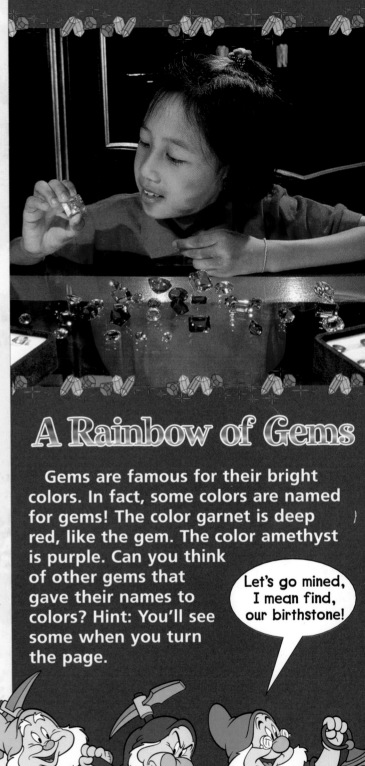

A Rainbow of Gems

Gems are famous for their bright colors. In fact, some colors are named for gems! The color garnet is deep red, like the gem. The color amethyst is purple. Can you think of other gems that gave their names to colors? Hint: You'll see some when you turn the page.

Let's go mined, I mean find, our birthstone!

Some people say that aquamarines can make you brave!

January's birthstone is the garnet. Long ago, people thought that this deep red gem could prevent wounds. Travelers would carry garnets so they would be safe on the road. Garnets were even said to prevent bad dreams!

February's birthstone is the amethyst. This rich purple jewel is said to help people think clearly and to chase away bad thoughts! Amethyst was also once thought to cure headaches and toothaches.

March's birthstone is the aquamarine. The name of this pale blue stone means "seawater." People once thought it could protect them from their enemies—and from shipwrecks!

Some birthstones, such as rubies, are very rare and cost a lot of money. Others are more common. But they are just as pretty.

Where do these jewels come from? Most jewels are mined—they are dug out of the ground.

JANUARY

GARNET

FEBRUARY

AMETHYST

MARCH

AQUAMARINE

They are special forms of minerals that are found in rock.

One birthstone—the pearl—doesn't come from the ground. Pearls form inside oysters! Oysters live in the sea, and that's where pearls are found.

You won't find a pearl in a mine!

A grain of sand got inside this oyster's shell. The oyster coated the sand with smooth, shiny layers. Now it's a pearl!

April's birthstone is the diamond. This glittery gem is the hardest material in nature! Diamonds are also expensive. But it's said that a diamond loses its value if it isn't given to someone with love.

May's birthstone is the emerald. A perfectly clear, deep green emerald is one of the rarest of all gems. This stone is said to give its wearer good health and good luck.

June's birthstone is the pearl. The pearl is called the "queen of gems." It has a soft, natural glow. Pearls need no polishing to shine! Most pearls are white. But there are gray, yellow, pink, and even black pearls.

APRIL
DIAMOND

MAY
EMERALD

JUNE
PEARL

All this gem dust is making me sneeze!

July's birthstone is the ruby. These rich red jewels stand for life and love. Fine rubies are rare and very valuable. Maybe that's why the ruby is often called the "king of gems."

August's birthstone is the peridot. This green gem forms inside volcanoes! In Hawaii, peridot is said to be the tears of Pele, the goddess of volcanoes. Peridot is said to help its wearer think clearly and act kindly.

September's birthstone is the sapphire. People once thought that deep blue sapphires had many powers. These gems were said to bring wealth and health. They were even thought to protect people from poisonous snakes!

Miners must know what to look for when they hunt for gems. Most gems aren't pretty and sparkly when they are in the ground. It takes a sharp eye to spot the rough stones as they appear in nature.

JULY

RUBY

AUGUST

PERIDOT

SEPTEMBER

SAPPHIRE

After a gem is mined, it must be cut and polished. Then its beauty can shine for everyone to see. When the gem is set into a piece of jewelry, it is ready to become a gift for a lucky someone's birthday!

Hrrmph! I still haven't found my birthstone. Maybe I need a turquoise good luck charm!

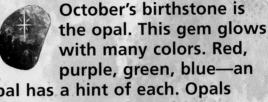 October's birthstone is the opal. This gem glows with many colors. Red, purple, green, blue—an opal has a hint of each. Opals were once thought to improve eyesight. They were also said to help blond hair stay blond!

November's birthstone is the topaz. This deep gold jewel glows like the setting sun. Topaz stands for loyalty. People used to think it could cure sickness and protect people from magic.

December's birthstone is the turquoise. This beautiful blue-green stone is often used in American Indian jewelry. It has long been thought to bring good luck. Turquoise is also said to be a charm against falling from a horse!

OCTOBER

OPAL

NOVEMBER

TOPAZ

DECEMBER

TURQUOISE

THE TREASURE HUNTERS

The Lost Boys were bored. They had played Follow the Leader with Michael and John. They had played Pirates and Pan with their pretend swords. They had stomped through swamps and swung through trees. But now. . .

"There's nothing to do," Slightly yawned.

"We need a new game," said Tootles.

John thought for a minute. "I know! Let's have a treasure hunt!"

That woke up Slightly—and all the other Lost Boys.

Little Michael jumped up and down. "Yes, John!"

The Lost Boys crowded around John and Michael.

None of them saw Mr. Smee sneaking up through the trees behind them.

"I'll make a map to the treasure," said John.

The Lost Boys cheered. This sounded like fun!

John took a piece of paper and some colored pencils and went off into the woods. The Lost Boys started to follow him, but Michael stopped them.

"No peeking!" he said.

The Lost Boys grumbled a little, but they sat down to wait for John to come back.

Mr. Smee hurried back to Captain Hook's ship. "A treasure! A treasure!" Mr. Smee said gleefully. "Oh, Captain Hook will be happy to hear about this! Ho, ho! Yes, he will!"

Captain Hook *was* happy to hear about it. "Any treasure in Never Land is *mine*, Smee," he said. "We'll get that map and that treasure!"

Smee danced a sailor's jig. Hook conked him on the head. "Get back to the rowboat. We're going ashore."

John walked slowly through the
forest. First, he had to think up some kind
of treasure for the Lost Boys to find. That was the
hardest part. Once he found that, drawing the map
would be easy.

He sat down on a log to think. "Treasure," John said
aloud. "Silver. Rubies. Gold." A bee buzzed past his
head. John started to wave it away, but the bee wasn't
interested in him. As John watched, the bee headed
straight for the hollow of a tree. "Gold," John said
again. He smiled.

Standing on his tiptoes, he could just see inside the tree. And what his eyes couldn't see, his nose and ears told him. There were bees buzzing inside the tree. There was a sweet smell coming from inside the tree. There had to be a honeycomb inside.

A honeycomb with golden honey in it!

"That's a pretty good
treasure," John decided. John and the
Lost Boys had once seen a beekeeper at work, so they
knew how to get the honey without getting stung.

John walked back through the woods. He drew his
map as he went. Then he added a clue: *Reach for the
treasure carefully—its guards are fierce as they can be.*

John laughed. "They'll have fun figuring this out."

Suddenly a hand clamped over his mouth. Mr. Smee
pulled John behind a tree.

"We'll take that!" said Captain Hook as he grabbed
the treasure map. "So kind of you to do all the work."

John struggled, but soon Smee had him tied to the
tree with a rag around his mouth. "Don't worry," he
said, patting John on the shoulder. "The Lost Boys will
know how to find another lost boy."

Hook and Smee gleefully set off after the treasure.

The Lost Boys were bored again. "Shouldn't John be back by now?" asked Tootles.

"Yeah. How long does it take to make a treasure map?" asked Slightly.

The Lost Boys started toward the woods.

"No peeking," Michael reminded them.

Slightly stopped. "Well, we can't peek if we don't know what we're looking for, can we?" He looked around at the Lost Boys.

Michael figured Slightly was right. And he wanted to
go with the Lost Boys. "All right," he said.

The Lost Boys cheered and ran into the woods. The
first thing they found was John.

Slightly untied the rag around his mouth.

"Hook took the treasure map!" John said.

"He'll find the treasure—*our* treasure!" cried Tootles,
and he stamped his foot.

The Lost Boys were ready to
run off, but John stopped them.
"Wait," he said. "I have an idea."
John led the Lost Boys close
to the honey tree. Smee and
Hook were trying to figure
out the last treasure clue.
"Oh, no!" John
shouted. "Hook has
found the treasure
tree!" He pointed to
the honey tree.
"You're too
late!" Hook said as
he smiled his very
nastiest smile. He
boosted Mr. Smee
up into the tree.
Mr. Smee reached
in—and got a
handful of honey.
"Oh, sticky, sticky,
sticky!" said Smee as

he tried to shake the honey off his hand. It splattered all over Hook's coat. Then the tree began to buzz.

Suddenly the bees came pouring out of the tree. They chased Hook and Smee all the way back to their rowboat.

When the pirates were gone, the boys cheered.

Slightly picked up the treasure map that Hook had dropped. "Reach for the treasure carefully—its guards are fierce as they can be," he read. He looked over at the tree. "I think those guards are gone."

"But the treasure's still there!" Michael clapped.

John carefully took the golden honeycomb out of the tree. The Lost Boys carried it back to their hideout and made a sticky-sweet mess.

Some time later, the bees buzzed back to their tree and began making more honey.

And aboard a certain pirate ship, a bee-bitten Captain Hook drank a cup of tea—without honey!

Tinker Bell's Wand

Sprinkle some magical Pixie Dust with Tinker Bell's wand—and soon you'll be spreading magic all around!

What You Need

Construction Paper

Scissors

White Glue

Glitter and Markers

Drinking Straw

Clear Tape

Curling Ribbon

1. Cut out two stars from construction paper.

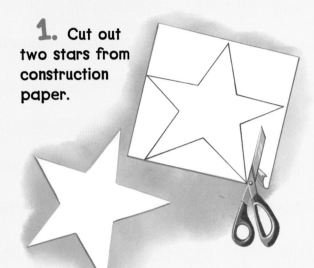

2. Tape the straw to one of the stars. Then place the other star over the straw, and tape the two stars together.

3. Color both sides of the star with your markers. Spread glue over one side of the star. Sprinkle glitter on it. Do the same to the other side of the star.

4. Curl the ribbon. Tie it around the straw near the bottom of the star. Wave your wand and begin granting wishes!

Crazy About YO-YOS!

Kids can do all kinds of tricks with yo-yos.

Up, down, up, down—I'm getting dizzy!

Have you walked the dog? Milked the cow? Rocked the baby? That's not a list of chores. Walk the dog, milk the cow, and rock the baby are some of the fancy tricks you can do with a yo-yo!

The yo-yo is a little toy that spins down a string and then comes back up. There isn't much to a yo-yo. It's just two wood or plastic disks. The disks are joined in the middle by a little bar. A string is tied to the bar with a slipknot and then wound around the bar. The free end of the string has a loop. The player slides the loop over a finger, usually the middle finger.

When the player throws the yo-yo, it unwinds along the string. And when it gets to the end of its string, the player gives it just the right little jerk. That makes the yo-yo wind itself back up and return to the player's hand.

The yo-yo is a very simple toy. It's also a very old toy. Children played with toys that were like yo-yos 3,000 years ago in China!

These yo-yoers are practicing two-handed tricks. Wow!

Yo! Want to Throw a Yo-Yo? Goofy Shows You How!

1.
Hold the yo-yo in your hand, palm up, with the loop of the string on a finger. Most yo-yoers use the middle finger. The loop should be as far back on your finger as possible.

2.
Curl your arm up toward your body. Bring your hand up until the yo-yo is about even with your ear. Now you're ready to do a yo-yo move called the throwdown.

3.
Lower your arm sharply. At the same time, open your fingers and flick your wrist to release the yo-yo. The yo-yo should fly out and down from your hand, unrolling along its string.

4.
When the yo-yo reaches the bottom of the string, turn your hand palm down. Give a slight upward tug on the string—and the yo-yo will climb back up to your hand.

The yo-yo's popularity has gone up and down over the years. But today kids are crazy about them! You can do lots of fancy tricks with yo-yos. There are tricks using two hands, and tricks you do with teams. And at yo-yo contests, people try to outdo each other with new and more difficult tricks.

The yo-yo may have more ups and downs in the years ahead. But this toy seems sure to keep coming back!

Not all yo-yos are just plain disks. Today a yo-yo may be shaped like a cookie, a basketball, a heart, or even a bowling ball.

DID YOU KNOW?

Did you know that yo-yos have gone into space? Astronaut David Griggs took a yo-yo on a space shuttle flight in 1984. That was a "high point" in yo-yo history!

Animal Lullaby

Three little wrens cuddle up to sleep on a tree branch.

Just like you, animals need to sleep. Sleep lets them rest and get ready for a new day. But you may be surprised at the bedrooms that some animals choose. It seems that animals can nod off almost anywhere!

Do animals dream when they sleep? Some do. But what animals dream about is anyone's guess!

A tree branch makes a good bed for a sleepy leopard, too.

A polar bear can sleep on ice. But this cub has a warmer bed: Mom!

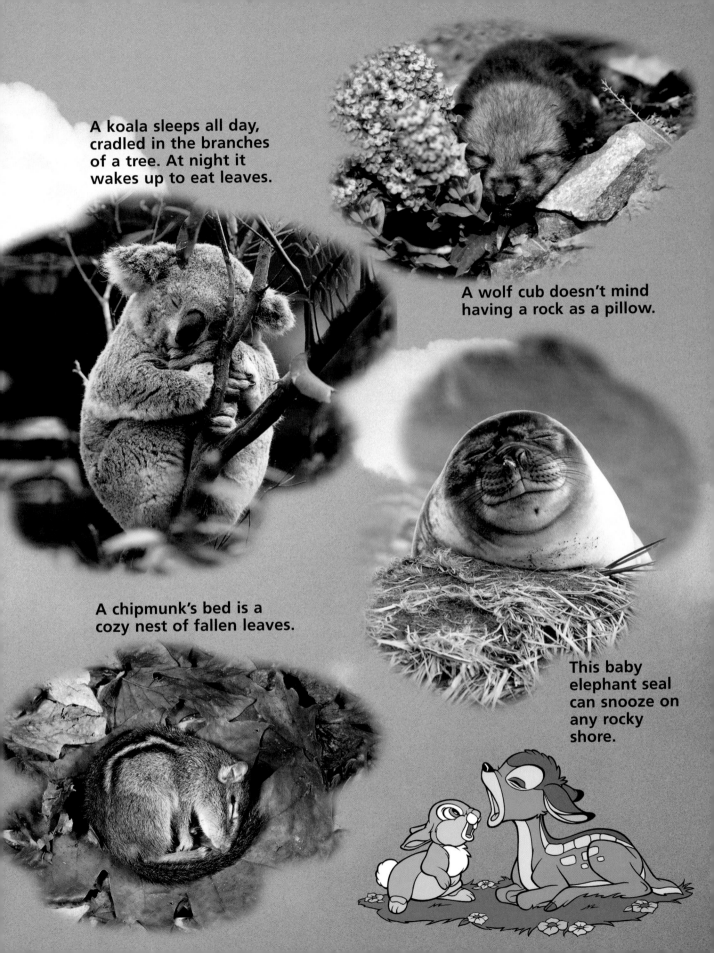

A koala sleeps all day, cradled in the branches of a tree. At night it wakes up to eat leaves.

A wolf cub doesn't mind having a rock as a pillow.

A chipmunk's bed is a cozy nest of fallen leaves.

This baby elephant seal can snooze on any rocky shore.

The Magic of Friendship

Once upon a time, there was a poor stonecutter named Mickey. He cut and carried stone to build cottages and stables, shops and fences. Mickey didn't mind not having much money, but he *did* mind the long and lonely hours he spent each day.

"I wish I had a friend," he sighed, cutting up a large boulder. Pieces of rock lay all around him. One stone stood out. It was an odd shape and sparkled in the sunlight. Mickey picked it up.

"Gosh, what a pretty rock!" he exclaimed, putting it in his pocket. "I will place it in the stone walk that leads to my house."

A little while later, Mickey heard a cry for help. He dropped his tools and ran out from behind the boulder. What did he see? It was Big Bad Pete trying to rob two ladies from the village.

"Oh, no!" Mickey gasped. The two ladies were Minnie and her wealthy Aunt Clarabelle. Quick as a wink, Mickey ran toward them and yelled at the robber. "Get away from those ladies this instant!"

Big Bad Pete just looked at the little stonecutter, a smirk spreading across his face. "Why should I?" he growled. The big crook loomed over Mickey.

Mickey thought, *I wish I could scare Big Bad Pete off.*
Just then, the rock Mickey had placed in his pocket
jumped out and bonked Pete right on the foot.

"Ow, ow, ow!" cried Pete. He hopped away, moaning
and carrying on.

Mickey turned to Aunt Clarabelle and Minnie. "Are
you ladies all right?" he asked them.

"Oh, yes," Aunt Clarabelle replied gratefully. "Thank
you for saving us from that horrible Pete fellow. Please
let me reward you for your bravery."

"Gosh, ma'am, it was nothing." Mickey blushed. "I don't want a reward. But if you happen to have work for a stonecutter, I'd gladly let you pay me for that."

"Brave, modest, and humble, too!" Minnie chimed in. She gave Mickey a warm smile. Mickey thought it was the prettiest smile he had ever seen.

"I do believe the wall around my house could be two feet higher," Aunt Clarabelle said.

Mickey picked up his sparkling rock and put it back in his pocket. Then he whistled all the way home. He was happy to have more work. He was even happier that he would be near Minnie. She seemed so nice.

When Mickey got back to his cottage, he took the rock out of his pocket. To his amazement, it began to glow in his hand.

"What do you wish?" the stone asked him.

"I-I-I beg your pardon?" Mickey replied.

"I am a magic stone," replied the glowing rock. "You released me from the boulder, and in exchange for my freedom, I will grant you three wishes. Your first request was granted when you wished to scare off that robber."

"So that means—" Mickey began.

"I will grant you two more wishes," finished the magic stone.

Mickey went inside his little cottage and sat down at the table. He placed the stone in front of him and stared at it.

"What do you desire?" the stone asked.

Mickey thought for a moment. "Can you give me a friend?" he wondered.

"The power to make a friend is yours alone," the rock answered. "But I *can* give you mountains of gold, a chest of jewels, or a castle filled with servants."

"I'm going to Minnie's tomorrow," Mickey told the stone. He looked down at his tattered clothes. "And I do wish I had something nicer to wear."

The next day, Mickey tucked the magic stone into his pocket. He arrived at Aunt Clarabelle's looking especially handsome in his brand-new outfit. Minnie certainly seemed to notice, and she gave Mickey another one of her lovely smiles.

Mickey tackled his work with newfound energy. In no time, Aunt Clarabelle's wall grew higher and higher. At lunchtime, Minnie brought him some cheese and bread and a cold glass of apple cider.

Best of all, she sat with him while he ate his feast! Minnie was so easy to talk to. It didn't seem to matter to Minnie that Mickey was a simple stone-cutter. "We would be pleased if you would join us for supper," Minnie told him.

Mickey went back to work and soon completed the wall. As the sun began to set, he washed up at the well. His heart leaped at the idea of seeing Minnie again. *I wish I had some flowers to give her*, he thought. Instantly, a beautiful bouquet appeared in his hand. He hadn't meant to use up his last wish on the flowers, but he was pleased nonetheless. "Thank you, magic stone," he said out loud.

That evening, Aunt Clarabelle's house was filled
with conversation and laughter. Aunt Clarabelle could
see how well her niece and the stonecutter got along.
"Would you please come back tomorrow and repair
the chimney?" Aunt Clarabelle asked. "I'm afraid it
will fall down if someone doesn't fix it soon."

"Of course!" Mickey happily agreed. As he was leaving, he pressed the magic stone into Minnie's hand. "I want you to have this," he told her, "because it's bright and sparkly, just like you."

"Thank you," Minnie said softly. "I'll keep it always."

As Mickey walked home that night, he realized that his fondest wish *had* come true. He had a best friend at last!

Hungry Plant

Lots of animals eat plants. But did you know that some plants eat animals? It's true! These strange plants trap insects for dinner.

Venus's-flytrap The leaves of the Venus's-flytrap look a lot like flowers. Each leaf ends in two flaps that face each other, like the pages in an open book. The flaps are a pretty red, and they are covered with sweet nectar.

Insects are drawn to the sweet-smelling leaves. But when an insect lands on a Venus's-flytrap leaf, it is trapped. Snap! The flaps close around the insect. It can't get out. The plant has caught its next meal.

Poor Ant

These plants are always hungry—just like I am!

A bee zooms in on a pretty sundew.

Sundew The sundew fools insects with fake flowers, too. Its leaves are covered with red hairs. The hairs are tipped with blobs of shiny, sticky goo. To bees and other insects, the sundew's leaves look just like flowers. But the leaves are really traps.

When an insect lands on a sundew, it is caught in the sticky goo. The red hairs bend over the insect. It can't get away. Then the leaf makes juices that break down the insect's body. The plant soaks up its meal.

The bee lands. It's stuck in sundew goo!

Leaf hairs bend over, trapping the bee.

Pitcher Plant It's easy to see how the pitcher plant got its name. Each plant has a little pitcher, filled with water. The pitcher is an insect trap!

Insects are drawn to the pitcher's sweet smell. They land on the pitcher's rim. But the rim is slippery. The insects fall in, and then they can't get out. The inside of the pitcher is covered with stiff hairs that point down. This keeps the insects from crawling up. They fall into the water at the bottom of the pitcher. There they break down into insect "soup" for the plant!

The pitchers of a pitcher plant are tube-shaped leaves. Insects go in, but they can't climb out.

Bladderwort The bladderwort is a water plant. It floats in lakes and ponds. The plant's yellow flowers stick up out of the water on tall stems. Under the water, the plant is covered with tiny air-filled sacs, called bladders. The sacs help the plant float. They are also insect traps.

Water fleas and other little water insects come to the bladderwort looking for food. When one of the insects brushes against a sac, the sac springs open. Water rushes into the sac, and the insect is sucked in. Then the trap closes. The insect is caught, and the bladderwort has a meal.

The bladderwort's flowers are above the water. Its tiny bladders are under the water. Here you can see how an insect is trapped in one of the plant's bladders.

Catch the Wind

Take a walk on a windy day. The wind pushes you along. It makes flags wave and kites fly. It sends bits of paper racing down the sidewalk. Maybe it even blows your hat away! Wind can be very strong. How can we use the wind's power? One way is to use windmills to catch the wind and put it to work.

A windmill is like a giant pinwheel. When you blow on a pinwheel, its blades spin. In a similar way, when the wind blows against the blades of a windmill, those blades spin. The spinning blades turn a bar in the windmill. And the turning bar runs a machine.

Long ago, people used windmills to grind grain and pump water out of the ground. Now there are special windmills that use wind power to make electricity. Lots of these windmills stand together in wind farms, like the one shown here. Wind farms help bring electricity to many homes— maybe even yours!

What Makes the Wind Blow?

Wind is simply air that is moving. What makes air move? Heat and cold give air a push. Here's how: The sun warms the Earth, but some places get warmer than others. The air above those places grows warmer, too. As air warms, it rises. Colder air then moves in to take its place. That moving air is wind. Air moves—and wind blows—all over the world.

This wind farm in Japan gets the most from the wind. It has 20 windmills stacked together!

These lovely old windmills are in Holland. Holland is famous for its windmills.

This windmill looks like a big pinwheel. Simple windmills like this were once found on many American farms. Farmers used them to pump water.

The blades of this old windmill in England catch the wind. But the base lets the breeze blow through!

Whoosh! Hang on to your hat!

The Last Laugh!

What did the mother ghost say to the baby ghost in the car?

Buckle your sheetbelt!

What happens to geese when they crash into each other?

They get goosebumps!

What's the difference between a bat and a fly?

A bat can fly, but a fly can't bat!

What do you call a kangaroo that watches TV all day?

A pouch potato!

What did the skunk say when the wind changed direction?

Ah, it's all coming back to me!

Where will the canary be when the lights go out?

In the dark!

Where does a 300-pound bear sleep?

Anywhere he wants to!